Cloudburst III

Poems by the Cambridge Pub Poets

Edited by
William Alderson and Colin Shaw

Chandler Press

2017

This book is dedicated to the people of Aleppo

Published by Chandler Press, Poppyseed Cottage, High Street, Stoke Ferry, Norfolk PE33 9SF
chandlerpress@mac.com

ISBN: 978-0-9568282-4-8

Set in Times New Roman and Gill Sans

Printed by Cambridge Printers Ltd, 1 Mercer's Row, Cambridge CB5 8HY
www.cambridgeprinters.co.uk

Contents

Foreword

The Cambridge Pub Poets have been meeting twice a year or so for nearly two decades, co-ordinated by Colin Shaw for ten years or more. All the poems in this collection are by current members of the group, apart from the guest appearance of Greg Freeman who read at our meeting in the winter of 2015.

In 2016 I had the good fortune to be asked to share with Colin in the organisation of meetings as they became quarterly, and so I have also had the pleasure of sharing the editorial work on this anthology.

The range of poetic styles in the group is wide, including work which is serious, humorous, formal and informal, short and long. Furthermore, a glance at the biographical notes reveals how diverse are the backgrounds of these writers.

At the same time, the wide range of topics echoes a common theme of managing loss and the possibility of renewal. We would expect poems about migration and war at the present time, but others about separation and bereavement seem to extend these issues into the domestic sphere. Even the more humorous pieces have a feeling of frustration, of trying to cope with a world not inclined to do us any favours.

In times of increasing uncertainty, there is a sense of writers questioning the past and looking for something firm to build on for the future. For me, it is the role of poetry, as an art, not only to document the present, but to try to understand it, and to offer such an understanding as a means for all of us to create a better and better informed future. I feel that these writers, each in their own way, are taking on that task.

William Alderson, December 2016

Jacqueline Mulhallen

Winter Migrants

Fly home, little bird.
Rain is falling.
Soon leaves will be falling too.

Fly across deep green valleys and huge rivers,
Over great mountains, peaked with snow,
Till you find the tideless shores of the inland sea.

Fly to the limestone island
Set in its turquoise waters.
It sheltered you as a fledgling.
Its warmth and beauty beckon
And welcome you now.

William Alderson

Silt Road

A slip of the ear and I'm in Samarkand,
   a road through wheat fields flushed with poppies, fluttering
   like silken banners over spears,
   shimmering heat which coalesces in
   a mirage of water and voices from the East.
   A ripple to the south the Romans marched
   where silting water settled to a bodied land,
   a causeway on a waterway that was,
   beside a waterway that was,
   as land and water struggled like a pod of eels.

The past, exotic tales, a foreign land
   are barely covered by the web of fields, each road,
   each dyke a silken thread drawn tight –
   the new land woven from the marsh and peat.
   Beside the Roman farms the eagle hovered, poised
   To stoop and kill, and still the kestrels glide
   The margins of the fields. The Fenmen fished and walked
   across the water melting into mist,
   the mist in which the drained land drowned,
   its liquid language foreign to Dutch engineers.

Of wealth and distant markets selling cloth
   this land knew nothing. Down the rivers and the roads
   drained crops and slaves and gold to feed
   the fashion of the times. The noble wives
   of Rome clothed naked wealth in fabric barely seen
   but worth its weight in gold; the Eighty now
   may strut the catwalk of their wealth but underneath
   the poor and refugees still flood, the stream
   of affluence is silting up,
   and though they've raised the banks, the water rises still

The merest tissue of a Chinese moth
flew over Caesar's triumph, but these banners brought
Rome down. Luxuriant display
did not feed armies, farmers or the land;
the picturesque does not pump water. These fields grew
fruitful by the plough and those who labour;
with foreign tongues or from the East, they share one truth:
the Silk Road is a mirage stealing joy
from poppies, sustenance from wheat.
Like us, on leaving Nordelph, Silt Road shrugs it off.

Janet Wright

Travels: An African Odysseus

In Greece – famous for epic voyages
and sailors who found the long way home from Hell,
clinging to wreckage or at least to hope,
buoyed up by the cracking tales they'd have to tell
of nymphs and monsters, to grandchildren not yet born –

today, on this sunny quiet Aegean beach
tourists write postcards home, licking their fingers,
stippling their words with juice from a sun-warmed peach,
take ferry rides and splash in the sparkling waves,
relax with a cool drink and some local fruit,
their weary travails and troubles left on hold
at home, with work clothes and the long commute

while unnoticed, as they watch the sun set, passes
an African Odysseus on the shore
(two thousand miles from a home he gladly left
with no idea what fortune held in store
after that fearful, crowded, seasick voyage)
offering his timeless freight of contraband,
illegal toys and beaded trinkets, hoping
to gain a foothold in this promised land –
not forced return, more work for the trafficker's fee
and another ordeal on that hated sea.

Jacqueline Mulhallen

Hungarian Border

The little girl weeps.
She is frightened by the violence, the noise, the fierce police,
The hatred – for her.
Three years old and she has seen it all!
They fled from guns and bombs and gas
And thought themselves in sight of safety.
Bearing her brother on his shoulders,
Her father takes her by the hand.
They turn away from the barbed wire.
They trudge.
A long winter settles on Europe.

Colin Shaw

Remembrance Day

They come on wheels,
the grim old soldiers,
granite faces like
fixed bayonets.
They trail their own memories
of lost comrades-in-arms
in the murderous mayhem
of beach or bridge
where poppies grow,
as they salute the memorial.
Who would want to
face these merciless
warriors on the field of blood?
Their cascades of medals
were their shields and spears
in Agincourts new.
How could they not
triumph in battle untriumphant?
When these few pass,
will new veterans spring
from the red soil they sowed
with dragon's teeth
to be our bright armour?

Paul Sayles

Serviceman's Wife

And the serviceman's wife, she said,

'You know what the news is?
I'm smothered in bruises',
And I don't care if he doesn't come home,
I don't care if he doesn't come home,
I don't care if he comes back dead.

'Cos when he comes home he takes to his bed,
He has nothing to say except 'I've got a bad head',
And when he's at home sudden noise makes him jump,

And the kids won't go near him for fear of a thump,

I don't care if he doesn't come home,

I don't care if he comes back dead.

The news makes him weep,
He shouts in his sleep.
I know where he's been,
But not what he's seen,
I don't care if he doesn't come home,
I don't care if he comes back dead.

I can't live with his terror, his stress and his fear,
There's nothing for me I can't get near,
And when it's time to go back, he can't say goodbye,
He can't hold me tight, can't meet my eye,
I don't care if he doesn't come home
I don't care if he comes back dead.
But don't send him home broken, damaged or maimed,
Just send him back dead,
And I'll just take the pension if it's all the same,
To you.

Greg Freeman

A Foreign Wood

The empire called for more men,
and they came.
Shipped from sub-continent
to western front,
Gallipoli, Mesopotamia, East Africa,
largest volunteer army in the world.

They weren't ready for the cold;
couldn't understand new officers
when theirs were slain. Some wounded,
shipped to England, died and were buried
in a corner of a foreign wood
with Muslim honours, near a mosque,

among the sentry birch and pines.
Undisturbed for decades,
then came vandals.
The soldiers were exhumed;
monument, arches, minarets,
domed gateway remain.

Remember them and their memorial,
when leaves cling on
in November wind,
magpies, crows call through the trees.
It's time to dig again the mossy turf,
create a garden; bury war, unearth peace.

*A burial ground for Muslim soldiers at Woking has been
turned into an Islamic peace garden.*

William Alderson

Selling Bombs
As supplied by Cameron, Fallon, Benn & Co.

This year we're going to gift-wrap all our bombs,
add season's greetings, ribbons, fancy bows,
and promise to deliver them by Christmas.

We sell traditional gunpowder black,
uranium grey and phosphorus white (quite chic),
and promise to deliver them by Christmas.

They won't come with the usual post –
our military supply them all by jet or drone,
and promise to deliver them by Christmas.

We guarantee that all your friends (or enemies)
will greet our bombs with wild cries of surprise,
and promise to deliver them by Christmas.

Our bombs are ethical, so don't complain –
we have a motto "Peace and goodwill to men",
and promise to deliver them by Christmas.

Anna Lindup

Breast Scan

Today I served up breast
On a plastic plate for SHE
Today it was breast on a plate
A menu for Nursie to see.

Breast on this plate please!
(She treats me like a dirk)
Breast on this plate please!
(It barely fits - will it work?)

Breast on the plate is served
Breast on the plate is ready
Chicken or turkey today?
Don't move! Breathe in! Hold steady!

So...Breast is ready, wohay
Llama or kangaroo?
Ostrich? Osprey? Vulture? Rabbit?
My breast is served up today

The problem with breasts, Nursie says
Is whether you've got the right shape:
Model breasts are loose and pendulous
Those aren't yours! - that's incredulous!

Had a model breast this morning
Do I want to know its size?
Large and long and pendulous
I understand – bigger is wise.

The best shape for Breasts – women wake, stay alert
The best shape for scanning so it doesn't hurt
The best shape for THEM is NOT the pert
Thanks a bunch – God it hurt!

Compressing begins and breathing hurts.
The long and loose are pain free!
You don't feel a thing UNLESS YOU ARE PERT
Don't move! She screeches with glee

Today I went for a scan,
Was upright firm and still
I placed my breast upon the plate,
My legs bent so,
Weight on the front,
Neck to the right
Hold handle tight
Lean back – shoulder front!
Grab left breast away!
Don't move!

I went for a scan today.

Natania Goldrich

Painting of a performance poem

Dave Hall

Answers

Google can answer
All of my questions, except
Why don't you pay tax?

York Winter Haiku

The moneyer struck
a replica coin for us
in Jorvik: Dane geld!

Metamorphosis
from an original idea seen in graffiti on a toilet door

Fallen petal, still;
Lit by sunshine, stirs, flies off;
Oh! a butterfly.

Silent Night
Zen haiku for Christmas

- - - - -
- - - - - - -
- - - - -

Mike Roe

Man On Top

Are you lonely up there in your cab in the sky
at the top of your tower-crane, there where birds fly?

When you idly gaze down upon the world every day
do you feel like the creator of all you survey?

When you're not pulling levers up there in the cloud
do you sing to yourself outrageously loud?

When a strong wind blows, does it create some unease
that your cosy warm nest sways around in the breeze?

Do you ever get dizzy looking down from that height,
and afraid that your crane will collapse on the site?

And what arrangements do you have for the loo?
How do you manage? What do you do?

When your day's work is over and your shift is at end,
how many minutes will it take to descend?

And when you're back down on the ground, is it a pain,
knowing that tomorrow you've got to climb up there again?

Paula Holt

Build Your Own Gingerbread Christmas Tree
Everything You Need Is In This Box

A friend – who 'doesn't like gingerbread' –
Was given this for Christmas
By a distant and inconsiderate relative,
So thought she'd pass it on to me
Because obviously, it would be so much fun for the kids
And, of course, for me, being a creative type.

The box sits ominously above their eye-level, catching mine,
Until the night before she's due to call again.
I like to warn the kitchen that I am heading its way,
To carefully plan and prepare myself for a protracted battle.
To be certain I'm ready for any trick it can pull.
I take out the instructions with trepidation.

When I find the start, there are two lists:
The first is the contents of the box;
The second is 'The other things you will need.'
I rapidly conclude that everything I need is NOT in this box
And the English has been translated by an alien
Who can neither spell, speak nor count

Unless certain steps have been specifically missed out
To test my patience further.
They provide: apparently stackable gingerbread stars
To form the tree; a white powder,
That I'm convinced you would need to snort
Before it started looking like green icing;

A piping bag (yeah, right); and candy baubles,
Clearly carcinogenic judging by their psychedelic colours.
One of the 'not in the box's
Is an 'electric mixer'. I am confused.
Do they mean a food-processor?
I have one in a cupboard somewhere.

19

Or do they mean a hand-held electric whisk,
Which I've seen on telly, but don't possess.
But if they meant a whisk they'd say 'whisk'
Or beat. Wouldn't they? Not mix.
But if they mean mix surely a fast arm is good enough?
I unearth the food-processor

And find it has an alternative double-whisk head,
Which I attach. The on button is horrifyingly loud,
So I presume it works.
"What are you doing?" my husband asks,
Knowing my sworn stand-off with the kitchen.
"Gingerbread Christmas Trees" I say. He thinks I'm swearing.

In the morning, I stuff the kids full of wholesome things
Then banish breakfast and announce:
"Oh look, a build your own Gingerbread Christmas Tree.
Doesn't this look fun?
You put the gingerbread stars in order of largest first
And I'll whip up some icing to stick them into a stack."

The instructions say 'take care, icing sets quickly',
So I hurtle into action mode,
Pour the packet into the processor
With pedantically measured half-teaspoons of water
And wrestle the component plastic parts shut and sealed
While the safety-catch tries to over-ride my mania.

I succeed in starting the machine,
The cat leaps 12 foot, making a hole in the ceiling,
The baby pulls his 2-second accusatory stare, like an alarm
system bleep
Before issuing a non-stop catastrophic wail
And I shut my eyes and count,
Ignoring the increasingly violent noise and shaking of the
mixer.

When I open my eyes, the children are staring at me.
"The stars won't stack, Mummy, they keep falling over.
Can we eat the baubles?"
"The baubles? No, they're not edible sweetheart. Sorry."
They're looking suspiciously at the icing mix. So am I.
It seems the icing has set in a thin layer

On the bottom of the mixer.
The alternative whisk-heads meanwhile have become
Semi-detached and mangled themselves into a
Twisted-looking hedgehog with a perm.
Clearly, for the last thirty seconds,
I have in fact been whisking the whisk-heads

Sod the teaspoons, I add a cup of water
To the ring of ice and use the non-electric mixer –
My arm with a wooden spoon attached.
I pour the icing into the piping bag faster than it can pour out
Then drown the collapsed gingerbread heap
And the kids fling baubles at it.

I take a photo of the finished creation,
Then they ask to eat the biggest star first
I.e. the one at the bottom of this Christmas splat.
The great green gingerbread sneeze is rapidly demolished,
Leaving two small cheery green faces,
On hyperactive e-number bouncing bodies.

In the afternoon my friend arrives.

"Where's the tree? Did you make it?" she cries.
"They ate it," I say. "I've got a photo somewhere."
"Did you have fun?" "Loved it."
"I knew you would. I've got you another one."
AAAAAAAAAAAAAAAAAAAAAAAGH!

Colin Shaw

The Dinosaur

I see the wrecking balls
smash through red-brick walls
to scatter the Victoriana
into drops of heart-blood,
pumping the time-corpuscles
so that death comes quickly,
too quickly for historic sense.
What things are these that
go up in their stead?
Baubles of glass and bubble wrap
that won't last a hundred years.
Along the road strips of cardboard
and painted breeze-blocks
spring up called Starbucks,
Next which has no next
that can be inferred,
and Marks & Sparks cheek
by jowl with last-minute
DFS selling sofas on the almost
tick that are not for life.

Past these flimsy shacks
stream the metal boxes
that are traded in yearly
for newer, shinier boxes,
for no good reason.

Temporary is the name
of this game of unthrones,
turning me into the dinosaur
that I am, with no faith
in "progress" that isn't progress
at all, for what is found to be good
in God's world is that which
has peaked in perfection
and works adequately,
needing no replacing
until timely thought
has had its final say.

Paul Sayles

Jimmy the Parrot

She came in and said,
Jimmy the parrot is dead,
Jimmy the parrot is dead,
And he was.
He was lying down there,
With his feet in the air,
Because Jimmy the parrot was dead.

Well after 34 years,
She shed buckets of tears,
Because Jimmy the parrot was dead,
And to comfort her mind,
I resolved to be kind,
Because Jimmy the parrot was dead,

But when she started the dead parrot routine,
My resolve, sort of,
Dissolved,
And I said.

'He's not down there of his own accord,
Neither is he pining for the fjord,
He's dead,
Jimmy the parrot is dead.

I know that you are weeping,
But he is not resting or sleeping
He is dead, he is deceased, he is gone
Jimmy the parrot is dead'

She was most disconcerted,
When I held him inverted

But, Jimmy the parrot was dead

Then I went to the shed,
And rummaged a spade,
And we laid him to rest
Somewhere nice in the shade,
Because Jimmy the parrot was dead,
Then we stared at the cage,
Full of emptiness.
After 34 years,
Because Jimmy the parrot was dead.

Mike Roe

Kicked Out of Bed

I remember it well.

'Ted', she said, 'get out of my bed.'
Just like that, all of a sudden.
And she threw me out.
I ask you, what's more to be said?
She can be cruel, there is no doubt.

So now, I'm hanging out here with the others –
The dumb blonde with the unblinking eyes
And the darkie, that cool dude with the stupid grin
and the curly black hair,
And the crazy clown who wears colourful suits,
And big flat boots.

And just as my eyes begin to close
And I'm starting to doze,
She comes over and gives me a cuddle,
And takes me back to bed, saying 'Sorry Ted,
'I'm not being fair to my favourite bear'.

Janet Wright

Love and the Artful Dodger

I have my lover's heart and he has mine.
He's a toff, calls me his Cockney sparrow:
different, yes, but we get on just fine.

He worked (a bit) in some creative line.
I earned our keep while he studied late Pissarro.
I had my lover's heart and he had mine.

Then he dumped me for an heiress – what a swine!
I took a knife. The blade was long and narrow.
Devilish, yes, but I'd get on just fine.

Moonlight bedecked the knife with an evil shine.
I slipped it in their door-lock, chilled to the marrow.
I'd have my lover's heart as he had mine.

Their walls were hung with pricy stuff, a goldmine!
I took the best and piled it in a wheelbarrow.
Difficult, yes, but I got out just fine.

Fair exchange, I left him a little sign:
a lipstick heart, pierced by a bleeding arrow.
Delinquent, yes, but I'm getting on just fine:
I sold my lover's art, and he has mine.

Janie Westbrook

Her Blacksod Grass

Old Grass, black with winters'
Silent grasp,
Watches the chilling waters
below; washing over Her
naked body.
bare limbed She sleeps late
amid dark ivy;
in a dreamless mist,
in a stream without time.

Tired leaves, wet faced since
autumns' passing,
hear the rushing winds
arriving, and cling to Her
raw shaven scalp:

to keep Her warm,
to keep Her mulched 'till dawn.

And hibernating eyes
watch the still grey skies:
no sun-drenched warmth today.

Old grass, black with winter
turns, in the icy wind
to soil.
"Bury Me, Bury Me!"
She cries in rain and snow,
she cries at the beauty of
low light-white sun
on the swans; wet-dry wings

where the air's journey touches
soft water,
touches laughter,
blows past old leaves and
blacksod grass,
which
from her sentient body grows.

Marina Yedigaroff

George and Natalie

Have you been getting my messages?
I send them daily by bird
                    fox
                        ant
It's a slow post
In the summer I will send them by
                        sunset
                            and by swallows
I will stick stamps on passing pigeons
Shout your graveside reference to speeding geese
A new grave
The one that is restless
The one where the dogs softly growl.

Greg Freeman

The Poetry Lesson

He turned up pissed, fresh
from the pub: glazed face,
breathing beer, gazed at the boy
in the front desk, stroked
his blond shock of hair.
About him flew books,
duffel bags, hockey boots.
It was all such a hoot.

The ale wore off, he growled
for quiet; clutched
with nicotine fingers the Penguin
book of contemporary verse,
decades out of date.
He coughed and choked,
forgot where he was.
He read with passion,

youth and tears: Hardy,
Owen, Thomas, Hughes.
Some still chucked stuff,
guffawed uneasily.
But listen. If anyone asks,
if there was one teacher ...
His lesson was this:
bards, booze, cigs and blues.

Paula Holt

Tunes

There are faces in my history
That dance emotions on my skin.
If I were, by chance, to meet one of them again,
What would it do? To me and you?

We are in tune.
Our rhythms coincide and intertwine.
These old songs are a memory
That make me smile, fondly,

But do not set my heart
Beat.

Marina Yedigaroff

Zephyr

Summer was old and aching in her joints
Draping grey over the saturated greens
                sweet peas
                      old poppies
Almost dahlia time
And in you roll
               Invisible
                Vibrant
Soft as silk
A silken gale disguised as a perfect breeze
Frolicking up from the Bay of Biscay
You danced your blissful way
To mend a day too hot and far too dull
And blew on our hot faces
               and sinking hearts
You dishevelled the woods
Ypu played the air like a harp
Two days you stayed
             and played
And then flew
And brought rain
       we knew would come
          with a flick of your peerless hem.

Janie Westbrook

Burial

Your chosen patch against the fielded boundaries
Waits by our ropewalk hedge of hawthorn,
Spersed with sapling ash and daisy memories
The dry summer ground heaved up
By unknown shovels hidden
Behind stones and flowers wreathed against
Those straight sides so carefully cut:
Chalky, airily defying the depths:
Making a tight but comfortable fit,
A gravel bed in which to lie
Between high brook banks
As if the Granta hugs your side
& so to swim in her sparkling shallows
Minnows rise with the morning sun
And set to her shore of sandy sticks
and woven willows, drawn
Crawling tendrils ivy-twine between
The floating wood that sails across your name
Our bier-boat that bore you here has gone
Back to the barn; beached to bare the past
& passed by the toppling church
Whose silence stayed, grave hymns sung out,
Raising stoney limbs to pray amongst the Anglian clouds
Words reigning down to write the turf:
All stillness now and calm below
The whispered grass,
The sunshine dancing round the shadows
As water everlasting in the gravelled shallows
As you swim slowly arm over arm over arm
As you join the dry yard-down earth
Of your own sun-warmed Elysian Field.

Dedicated to my father Ronald William Westbrook 1924-2012
Spersed: sprinkled like a natural or random dispersement
(OED).

Biographical Notes and Acknowledgements

William Alderson has been published in two anthologies – *Cloudburst2* (Chandler Press, 2012) and *Poems For Peace* (Chandler Press, 2015) – and over 20 magazines, including *Acumen, Envoi, Orbis, The Rialto,* and *Poetry Salzburg Review.* He has been shortlisted or won prizes in several competitions. In 2016 he won a commission to write a poem for two voices performed in Peterborough. He is a letterpress printer and is hand-printing a range of poem cards available at http://williamalderson.wix.com/williamalderson.

'Silt Road' won second prize in the Fenland Poet Laureate Awards 2015.

Greg Freeman is a former newspaper sub-editor, and now News Editor for the poetry website Write Out Loud (www.writeoutloud.net). His debut poetry pamphlet, *Trainspotting,* was published by Indigo Dreams in 2015.

Natania Goldrich is a painter and professional singer.

Dave Hall studied biochemistry at Cambridge, and is now a technical translator, German to English. He was brought up in Malvern, an area associated with famous poets from the time of William Langland. His great influences are the Liverpool poets of the 60s and the Dymock poets, especially Edward Thomas and Robert Frost. None of which explains why he mostly writes haikus.

Paula Holt plays with numbers by day as an accountant for PriceWaterhouseCoopers, but finds the train journey to London an ideal space for writing poems. After doing English, Maths and Art A-levels, she edited the college magazine while doing a Maths degree. Four children later, she has painted a sky on her living room ceiling and a toilet roll on the bathroom wall to confuse unsuspecting visitors (don't worry there is a real loo roll on the other wall).

'Build your own gingerbread Christmas tree ... has been published in her ebook Comedy Poems for Cooking with Children by Poppyanna, *available from Amazon.*

Anna Lindup trained as an actress, performing on stage, film, radio and television. She has performed her own poetry at Glastonbury, London's Poetry Café and the Old Operating Theatre. She is a member of The Poetry Society and The Poetry Show.

Jacqueline Mulhallen has been published in two anthologies – *Cloudburst2* (Chandler Press, 2013) and *Poems for Peace* (Chandler Press, 2015). She was also commended in the 2014 ArtemisPoetry competition. She has published two books on Shelley – *The Theatre of Shelley* (OpenBooks Publishers, 2010) and *Percy Bysshe Shelley: Poet and Revolutionary* (Pluto Press, 2015). She also wrote and performed a one woman play *Sylvia* (1987, revived 2015) and two hander *Rebels and Friends* (1989) produced by Lynx Theatre and Poetry.

Mike Roe has had a lifelong interest in poetry, painting, cinema and literature. After early retirement as a Chartered Surveyor in a large local consultancy, he began eight years of intermittent solo travelling in South and Central America and Asia, armed with backpack and sketchbooks. Now he continues his love of the arts in several groups in the Cambridge area where he has lived for nearly fifty years. Has one book to his name - *A Collection of 35 Short Stories*.

Paul Sayles has 'always been a scribbler' of short stories, articles (mainly about fishing and politics) and so on. Poetry has been an abiding passion and he has recently started reading it again after a break of about 20 years. In a former life he was a social worker specialising in mental health and addictions. Nowadays he is an active local politician and a closet player of the accordion.

Colin Shaw is a foreign affairs journalist by trade, but he has been writing poetry on and off since the age of 11. He has published two collections – *Pomes* (1975) and *A Word In Your Beer* (Chandler Press, 2011) – and he is now working on his third collection. He is an Anglican Lay Minister, but doesn't always write 'holy' verse.

'Remembrance Day' and 'The Dinosaur', have been published in Reach Magazine.

Janie Westbrook went to art college and studied 3D Design; worked as a goldsmith in Spain and Bristol; then ran Children's Arts Workshops for many years. Now her son is at university, and she divides her time between Bristol and Cambridge looking after her mother and doing up her house. She occasionally writes a poem or two over a pint of real ale.

Janet Wright is a journalist but keeps an emergency poetry supply in her motorbike topbox. She has travelled the world with an anthology in her pocket. She didn't write poetry herself until she saw the potential for making haikus in headlines. Expanding from there, she found villanelles and sonnets harder to camouflage in print. Her work has been published in the *Poetry Trail* 2012 and Home collections by Paekakariki Press.

Marina Yedigaroff is a painter as well as a poet. She won the 1995 Woodland Press prize for poetry with her 16 page poem 'The Chartreuse Spring'. She has been published in various poetry magazines and in *Her Minds Eye* edited by Rachel Lever. She recently came third in the Fenland Poet Laureate Awards 2016. She lives in Ely.

Other publications by Chandler Press

Cloudburst2

The second collection of poems by the Cambridge Pub Poets, edited by Colin Shaw and Stephanie Shaw.　　**£5.00**
ISBN: 978-0-9568282-1-7

Poems For Peace

A collection of anti-war poems edited by Poppy Kleiser when she was the 2014 Fenland Poet Laureate.　　**£12.99**
ISBN: 978-0-9568282-3-1

A Word In Your Beer

The second collection of poems by Colin Shaw.　　**£5.00**
ISBN: 978-0-9568282-0-0

Poem Cards

Chandler Press also publishes a growing series of greetings cards designed, set and printed by hand on an Arab treadle press. The series includes poems by William Alderson and Colin Shaw, with one by Jacqueline Mulhallen forthcoming. Each card has a unique border design created using fleurons, the traditional printers' decorations.　　**£2.50 each**

Current poem card designs can be seen at
williamalderson.wixsite.com/williamalderson/poem-cards

All these publications are available from
Chandler Press, Poppyseed Cottage, High Street, Stoke Ferry, Norfolk PE33 9SF
chandlerpress@mac.com

Cloudburst III